The Pros
And Cons
Of Knowing
A Woman!

The Pros
And Cons
Of Knowing
A Woman!

Poetic Woman

To order additional copies of this book, contact:
Xlibris Corporation
1-888-795-4274
www.Xlibris.com
Orders@Xlibris.com
68258

CONTENTS

Dedication

This book is dedicated to every woman in the world that knows how to keep it real and when to be honest with their mate. But this book is also dedicated to all you haters out there in the world that doesn't know how to appreciate a good man or know when to mind your own business.

Chapter One

As everyday goes by in today's society you're not going to find a woman that knows exactly what a man wants. Knowing what a man wants comes with a chance of sometimes being very risky depending on who the person is. You have men that want to live the life of a thug. You have men that want to live the life of a player. You have men that want to be liars and cheaters. And you also have men that just want to be loved by only one woman.

Some men think of women as you lose one and another one will come along. But a man just wants to feel appreciated and wanted by someone. Some men just want to be with a mature woman. A woman who isn't going to be a gold digger. A woman that has some class to her personality style. A woman that has a little freak in her. A man just wants a woman that will cater to him at least four to five times out of a week.

As a woman myself at least I know what my man wants and that is all that matters. My man just wants to be happy. He doesn't want to argue at all. He just wants to be met at least half way. He wants to be treated with respect. He wants to be able to just say I love you and make me laugh. Impossible you might say to yourself. Even when something might be wrong.

Anything can be possible as long as two people have a set mind and know how to handle any obstacle. But when things are looked at as being one-sided then it might be time for someone to pack their bags and go.

For example, I know of a few relatives that didn't know what their partner wanted. Or they didn't know what they wanted out of life either.

So the deal is that they had to part their separate ways and go on to try and find someone that they are more compatible with.

You have cousin J.C. that took her boyfriend back even after he cheated on her. One reason is that he didn't take her to her senior prom in high school. He took someone else and made up a story that he was somewhere else. Next you have cousin T.B. that doesn't know how to treat a man or when to quit stealing. And you have cousin L.K. that doesn't know when to keep her mouth close and mind her own business. Because there is a time and place for everything.

It's like the saying goes if a good man came their way that they wouldn't know what to do with him. Or for that fact they wouldn't know how to treat him or keep him. First of all they shouldn't believe in everything that they hear. Because believing in he say she say gossip is what always seems to make something else go wrong. Another example, is when a woman knows what a man wants but he always expect to be catered to 365 days out of a year.

A prime example is how could two men be fighting and arguing over a girl and then she thinks that it is funny. She cuts her brother with a box cutter first and then she disrespects her own mother and aunts. She dropped out of high school and only needed half of a credit to graduate. She also targets married men and then their wife won't even know what's going on. Then you have another cousin that had a job making thirteen dollars an hour and the only thing that she knew how to do was be late. Not only was she late all the time but she gets fired for also stealing a pop.

Beside the fact is that I believe that if a person only knew how to mind their own business they wouldn't have anything to worry about. They wouldn't have to always be looking over their shoulder. Or they wouldn't have to carry a gun or knife to try to protect themselves. Honesty is what sometimes can break a person or make a person. Another thing that will break a person down is when you mess with their financial.

Some men want a woman that is going to get along with his family and friends. But you also have some men that want a woman to take care of them. A woman to take the wrap for them especially when they know that they already have two strikes against them. From a drug case down to letting him drive your car and have any man or woman in it that he wants.

There are always a few simple questions that every woman should ask herself when it comes down to a man or a lover. She should ask herself do I really love him? Does it matter what anyone has to say about our age differences? Will he abuse me if he has any liquor in his system? And is he a spoiled man?

If the answer is yes to the second and third questions then it is time to go. That's because he is expressing his true feelings to you. Because they say that a man will let a woman know how he truly feels when he is drunk. That's because when they're sober the only thing that some men think about is sex and that's mostly the young ones.

But if the answer is also yes to the first and fourth questions you might have a chance. A slim to nothing chance is better then no chance at all. Only because everyone makes mistakes. But when it comes down to making a mistake it comes a time to draw the line somewhere. Although both men and women take some things a little to serious. It is like all work and no time to play at all.

That is why sometimes knowing what a man wants can be risky. Because you have some men that are all about getting one thing. That one thing is called money or too much power and some men just want to use some women as a sex object. But when some women have them waiting for a long time before they give it up they think that they are getting it from some other man.

Then on the other hand you have some men that appreciate want their woman do for them.

A man might want his woman to bring him a dozen roses and a box of chocolates. A man might also want his woman to run his bath water sometimes. But I think that when a woman runs her man bath water then that might be a beginning of a happy marriage or relationship. That is if anyone doesn't come in between the middle of their relationship and try to throw things off track.

For example, if a woman knows that a man has a wife that is very sick what does she do? Does she take advantage of the situation and invite him over for dinner? Or does she just try to get straight to the point and just jump in bed with him? Because if that man was any kind of real man he would tell that woman that he has to be by his wife side at all times. Except for when he is working to take care of home. But when you have men that don't care who they sleep with in the end someone is going to end up hurt.

Every man and woman should think of life and relationships as it is not everyday that a good person comes my way. Do I want to have a happy life? Or do I want to die alone knowing that I could have been with Mr. Right?

A man that wants some alone time to himself isn't a man to worry about. It's not like saying that you have done anything wrong. Or maybe you might have and you're trying to find a way to cover up. But a man might just want some time to hang out with his boys. Although some women might take that the wrong way.

A man might only want you to fix him breakfast in bed after he had just made love to you the night before. It's like reading a man like an open book. But you can't always judge a book by its cover. Just like you can't always judge a man by the color of his skin. Some men just prefer to be treated fairly not like your house maid.

It's like whenever you find an insecure woman or man then it might be time to worry. Or just try to sit down and talk things out to see if maybe you can forgive and forget. Because an insecure person is a person that you always have to worry about what they're going to say next. You might say to yourself do I sit here and take everything that he or she is dishing out? Or do I go over the computer and find myself a blind date? Because some men would just look at porn for their own enjoyment. Then again they would watch some kind of sport.

Besides an unhealthy relationship with anyone is a sign. It is a sign that you didn't have a pleasant childhood. Or maybe you was an only child and no one wanted to play with you. You could have been married once before and then you decide to take your anger out on your second spouse.

If any woman doesn't know what her man likes or dislikes then it is time to talk. It is time to get to know your mate. To see how many things that the two of you have in common. Or to see how you can compromise when it comes down to what the other person wants.

Here is what a thug man might want from his woman. To go down on him and his friends and not have to be charged for it. Because you do have some women that will do anything for a quick dollar. They just claim to be faithful to their boyfriend while he is locked up. When really they are just trying to get their bills paid while trying to be satisfied. Because they might be tired of playing with their toys.

Sometimes it doesn't even matter if they're working as a crew manager at a fast food restaurant. I know of a girl that is like that. She has so many enemies that she tries to stay in the house when she gets off of work. As the saying goes don't quit your day job. But in her case I hope that she is wearing some kind of protection when she is in the bed with all of those men.

I see it as a woman that is willing to give herself to a total stranger is a woman that doesn't care. She doesn't care about her body or how long she might have to live. Or if she catches something that she can't get rid of. That's because some women are so use to being used by some men anyway. That they are on the verge of committing suicide. First they might take too many pills. Then they might shoot up. Finally if they are talked out of it they might have to be admitted to a mental institution. Because you have some women that think it is hard to find love.

Knowing what a man wants could also save a woman's life. She might think do I defend myself if something goes wrong? Or do I sit here and plot on how I'm going to kill him? Every man and woman doesn't act the same way if they're upset or depressed about something. That's because you have some women that know how to handle any kind of situation. They do anything that is possible to be able to see another day.

In life you have some jealous men and women. Some of them not knowing the right time to be intimate. Or when to report something to the police. That's because some men want a woman that knows how to take care of home first and then spend the rest of their time with you.

I also know what a man doesn't want. He doesn't want a woman that is going to walk all over him like a welcome mat. He doesn't want a woman that is very flirty. He doesn't want a demanding woman. He also doesn't want a woman without any kind of experience.

You have all types of men in the world but knowing what all of them want could give a woman a headache. For example I asked this man what does he want out of a woman here is what he had to say. He said that I want a woman that is going to let me breathe. I want a woman that doesn't want to accuse me of being with another woman when I am working. I want a woman that doesn't want to have sex as soon as I get home.

He also said that I want a woman that isn't going to send me a crazy text message. Here is what the text message said. I miss you I am sorry and I want some right now. So he told himself that man this girl is crazy. She is crazy because she is calling me all times of the day when she knows that I am working. I really don't want her is what he said. But I don't know how to tell her is what he also said. So the best thing to do is to tell her that you are not happy is what a fellow co-worker told him.

Although, his main problem is that he just needs to quit drinking before he comes to work. He comes to work when he feels like coming. And when he pretends to be short on cash he asks just about everybody for about five dollars. But the bad part about it is that he forgets to pay it back. He sometimes has to be reminded. Only because he needs help but he doesn't want to be told that he needs to go talk to a specialist of some sort.

Another prime example is that how do women try to stay faithful if their main squeeze is in trouble? Some women will go to someone for help. Someone that they can trust with their most inner thoughts and deepest feelings.

Some women might think that if a man cries that something is wrong with him. But sometimes a man can be just as emotional as a woman. He might be trying to express his true feelings for you. He might be asking for a second chance. He might have also just lost a loved one that he was close to. But I feel like you shouldn't have to down a man especially when he has just lost someone.

Here is what every woman should do when she gets out of bed in the morning. She should go to her man and ask him how does he feel this morning. She should tell him how much she loves him. She should fix him some lunch to take to work. And she should also ask him how his day was at work when he comes home.

Some women love the fact that their man can take them shopping for whatever they want. But you have some men that love it whenever their woman buy them a pair of shoes. I bet you didn't think that I would have a story for this situation too.

There was this boy that would buy this girl anything that she wanted. But all she had to do is go out with him. He would give her money if she wanted it. He would buy her shoes and clothes. He would get her hair and nails done. He would buy her those big stuff animals and a box of chocolates. But the deal is that she didn't like him at all. She wouldn't give him the time of day.

This is how a woman feels if another woman was to buy here man a drink. She might think that another woman is trying to take her man from her. She might also think that maybe it is his birthday. Or maybe they are just close friends.

In conclusion of knowing what a man wants is a woman that is a good listener. That's because there is nothing like a good listener. A good listener hears every little detail. They hear what needs to be improved down to what doesn't. They also hear if their mate is going to meet some other woman at a motel.

Chapter Two

As your fellow co-worker and associate I think that you should just stop worrying. You shouldn't have to keep worrying about who wants to fight you or break your windows over a man. Just because if he was any kind of real man he wouldn't have a problem telling that other girl that he only has eyes for you. But seeming as that he just doesn't mind getting out of the bed in the middle of the night and trying to deal with a whole lot of bickering.

You shouldn't have to fight over any man especially when he is already yours. Because either he wants you or he doesn't. Think of it as if he doesn't want me that there are plenty of other more fish in the sea. But in your case you shouldn't have to fight for a man that is already yours unless he brings drama along.

Although, if you want your relationship to be stronger just stop and think to yourself. Stop and think to yourself do I really want to be with this man? Or just we have a child together that he is trapped. Because no one is perfect at all. Everyone has their good and bad days. And their ups and downs. No one can have a perfect relationship or marriage at all.

Life and love isn't just the way that it use to be. That's because back in the 30s through the 60s love meant something then. You could go to sleep and leave your down open. You could go to a house party and not have to worry about anybody having to be shot. You could go skating and not have about who was liking who. That's because life just isn't the way that it use to be.

For example, back in the 60s if a man liked another man's woman they would fight instead of kill. Another example, is that men went to work while their woman stayed at home and took care of the kids and home. Also back in the 60s everybody was raising each others kids. Then if their parents thought that they deserved another whooping they got one when they got home.

Everyone has to look at life as it is too short and that tomorrow isn't promised to none of us. Either you are with a person for who they are. Or you are with a person for what they have. But think of it as what if they don't have a shiny dime to their name. Saying that they are totally broke. Do you expect to live off of just love or is it something else?

As your co-worker I believe that the only thing you should do is just try to shake it off. Because you shouldn't try to resolve anything with violence. That will only leave you in four possible places. In jail, in prison, 6 feet under or in the hospital. That's because you know that deep within your heart that you deserve to be treated with respect.

Every man should treat his woman like he would do his own mother. But that is why every woman should do a background check before they get to involved. You should ask to meet his parents and see how they act and then that would give you some kind of insight. And then you should ask yourself is this a family that I want to be involved with.

Then every woman should ask herself how many chances do I want to give him before I call it quits. Although if some women are with men for a long time they find it harder to let go. Then again you find other women that find it easier to get rid of man. This is what they might do. They might tell you that they have a headache or that they don't feel good at all.

Some women have so many excuses in the world for not wanting to be bothered with a man. Starting off with the excuse of his family not liking her. Then the excuse of not wanting to be intimate because it is that time of the month always. Or the excuse that she has slept with one of your friends before the two of even got together. Or maybe the excuse that she is saving herself for that special person. But the real deal with some women is that they are too afraid to let any man get too close to them.

Every woman should think to themselves that no man is worth being stressed out over. No woman shouldn't at all shouldn't have to wake up crying and wanting to take their problems to work. But this message is to my co-worker especially. I want you to stop and also think if you were to find someone else that didn't want to always argue and make you want to cry would it be too hard to believe? You should think of yourself as an independent woman that can have any man that she wanted. I mean as long as he is single and available.

Beside the fact at least you aren't a materialistic woman. A materialistic woman is a woman that says that she doesn't need a man to validate her. A woman that doesn't mind being alone. Someone who doesn't need a shoulder to lean on. But with some women they can be independent and have a man by their side. Because as the saying goes everyone has needs but some people are just in denial.

I just want everyone to know that I don't claim to know everything when it comes to two people being in a relationship. I believe that the best thing that any woman could do is just try to stay away from trouble. To not have very many female friends at all. Because females are each others enemies.

Although it is the majority of young females that are enemies with each other. That is why women shouldn't take their man around their friends or family for that fact. And another thing is that is why some married couples only hand around other married couples. Because some single people attract too much attention to a married man. I bet you are wondering how I know that.

I know that because a relative of mine use to take advantage of a married man while his wife was at work. She use to drive his van and have anyone in it that she wanted to be in it. But the bad part about it is that one day she was in the back seat of his van while his wife was in the front. And his wife just thought the both of them were just friends and nothing more. She use to always ask him for money to buy herself some food, something to drink or something to smoke. She is the kind of woman that goes looking for trouble.

It's like one female gets jealous of what another female has. She wants what she can't or maybe can have. For example, if a man takes his woman around his friends and leave you there for about 30 minutes then he trusts you. He trusts that you won't try to seduce his friends or that his friends won't flirt with you. Because some men are just wanna be players. That's only because some people don't think before they react.

It's not like saying that I watch too much lifetime or any other television show. But here's what I think that every woman should do when it comes down to a man. Not saying that every woman should listen to what I am about to say.

Although it doesn't hurt to always listen to what someone else has been through. That's because experience is your best teacher. Either you learn from it or someone suffers behinds it.

But as a young woman myself I found out that by being with an older man that it has its advantages. But in my sisters case she thinks that I am a bit crazy. But I am loving every moment of my life. Every moment spent alone with him is every moment cherished and remembered. The advantage is that by him being older that I have that I could learn from him.

Rule number one you should check out a man's background before you start getting really involved with each other.

Rule number two never let a man tell you that he loves you when the only that he wants is one thing. And then he might move on. That only applies to most young men.

Rule number three never take your man around your family or friends. Because they might want what you have because they are trying to find every little mistake you make and keep tabs on you.

Rule number four if you have a man that drinks then that's a sign. It's time to go is what that means.

Rule number five always give your man some breathing space. It is not always good to be breathing down his neck.

Rule number six admit when you are wrong to prevent any arguments from happening.

Rule number seven don't let your man go to a strip club to see another woman strip for him.

Rule number eight when someone talks about your man it is best for you to defend his honor only when he is right.

Rule number nine always keep your man happy and satisfied.

And the final rule is to keep his stomach full.

Every woman should look at life and relationships as give and take. You have to give a little and take a little. But life has its limits when it comes down to everyone. Some women just think that all that they have to do is just shake it off and go on with their lives. But for some women they say that it ain't that easy. They think to themselves well I have gave him so many years of my life and this is how he wants to repay me.

I just consider myself to be lucky to have someone in my life who is willing to teach me some things. Because I don't mind letting him teach me anything at all. But it is just up to me whether or not I want to listen so that I won't make those mistakes. But I think that some people just waste their money paying some therapist for advice to tell them how to make improvements on their relationship.

It's only because I believe in the fact that opposites attract. Because some women and men have a hard time trusting any man or woman. Due to the fact that they are tired of their feelings being hurt 80% of the time. They feel like they just want to be happy and they want someone who knows what it means to be happy also.

For example most women could be turned off by boredom. If that applies to you then it is either time to go or try to spice up your sex life. Because a man that is worth keeping is a man that is worth being honest to. But a woman just feel like she needs some kind of security.

This goes for just about any woman communication can be our biggest problem if we don't learn how to speak up. That's because some women are afraid of what might happen as a result of being open-minded. But here is what some of us fail to realize. Some women let what is between their thighs do all of their thinking for them.

I feel like some women are just use to being treated a certain way. They either don't want to change or don't know how to change. Some women are afraid of what a change or two might do for them. Some women might be afraid that it will be something to always expect.

For example take this situation and try to figure out what this person should do. If a woman thinks of her man all the time but doesn't want to wait on him because he is in prison what she should do? Should she wait for him or go get her needs fulfilled somewhere else? Do you think that she should send another man money in the same prison that her boyfriend is in? Do you think that her boyfriend believes that she is being faithful to him? What do you think that she should do when she gets caught in bed with another man by one of his family members? Do you think that honesty is one of her best characteristics? Because I believe that everyone is entitled to their own opinion about her when she already is well known in the streets.

She just thinks that it is okay to do what she does and then thinks nothing of it. She says that she is tired of her boyfriend family lying on her. She says that she is going to call it quits and break up with him. But she is the one that is doing everything wrong that is possible to think of. Although she is in denial. She told him that she was missing him and that she is being faithful to him. She also told him that she makes 500 dollars every week and that she is tired of having to put money on her phone to be able to talk to him. She also said that she enjoys having phone sex over the phone.

She is just one of those kind of women that a man wishes that he never met. She is one of those women that you could never make happy. That's because she feels like she has to try out every man before she is finally satisfied when she catches something she can't get rid of.

I admit that I have made a few mistakes myself back in the past. I have picked two wrong people to be involved with. I thought that I knew what love was. I thought that no one could tell me anything at all. I was that kind of woman that wanted to get to know a little bit about you. But I also knew when to keep my mouth closed. Until you made me mad that was.

I was also a very shy person in the beginning but I knew when I wasn't wanted or loved.

Let me leave you with these words to remember from this chapter. The best thing that any woman could ever have is her freedom. Because without freedom your life is just like a burning fire. Everything just goes up in flames and you regret even saying hi and introducing yourself to him.

Chapter Three

Real talk is that every woman yearns for a man to make love to them and then wake up to the sound of their voice the next day. Real talk is that a woman just wants to be able to feel safe around her man. She doesn't want to have to feel like she has to fight for her own life. She wants to be able to know that she can trust you even when you're not around her. Real talk is that reality bites and teenage girls coming up today just need to know when to mind their own business.

Some women feel like that no one can tell their child what to do. It's likesaying that they have to see it to believe it. Not believing in he say she say gossip. Real talk is when a man doesn't know his partner whereabouts. It's like knowing how long it takes to get from point a to point b.

For example, it's like if a woman tried to tell her father who he should or shouldn't date. Then she also tells him that he is messing around with the wrong bunch of people. That he should get out while he can. And his response was I am your father you aren't my parent. So she told him that you act like I don't exist and then you are always going around telling a whole bunch of lies.

The whole point of a daughter trying to tell her father who he should date is that she might feel left out. Being the fact that he was never there for her when she was coming up. But now that she is all grown up he feels like she has her own life to live. Whenever any holidays came around she felt like it would be just a waste to go see him. She also feels like it is time for him to step up and be a grandfather to his grandchildren. She even feels left out when he doesn't even remember her birthday and she is his only child.

Another example, is how does a man show his daughter that he cares for her? When he doesn't know how to love himself first. And then try to stay sober long enough to talk straight. A prime example is that a person that I knew felt like she had to go through another man's phone. The point is that they weren't even dating. But the fact is that even if you are dating or married that is the reason why you should trust your mate. But it also comes with a risk of starting an argument or even worse losing the best man that you ever had.

Real talk is that some women are just living in a fantasy world. They are living on cloud nine. They don't want to be told that they should stop dreaming. It's because some women are just wishing certain things would happen instead of doing something about it. Some of them believe that the grass is somehow greener on the other side.

Real talk is that some women would rather take their chances by being with a thug verses a real man. They somehow feel more protected with a thug. They feel like a thugs way of loving them is by back handing them. Or just because they are hustlers they figure that they want a man that knows how to make some quick cash.

For example, if a teenager told her mother that she was going to go to a basketball should she believe her? Maybe or maybe not. That's because she used a basketball game as an excuse to go see her boyfriend. Here is what she did. She skipped town for about three days and didn't nobody know where she was at. She also loves to wait until her mother goes to sleep just to sit outside in the front yard. She sleeps half the day away and then she tries to stay out all night.

Regardless of what a teenage girl or her mother does family is the first to judge. Although family isn't always the ones to be there whenever you might need a shoulder to cry on. Someone to tell your feelings to and someone that you expect would tell you some of their past experiences.

Family members are always the first ones to judge another family member because they are just jealous. They are jealous because they think that they know a bad person when they see one. It's like judging a book by its cover. But you have to get to know a person before you judge them.

I also believe that actions speak louder then words. But some women are just blinded by love. They would rather be a follower then a leader. They would rather take the wrap for a drug transaction. Verses to singing like a mockingbird at the time of trail.

Real talk is that some women feel like that they have to be intimate with a man in order for you to notice them. But real talk is that there are too many types of birth control in the world for anything to happen like catch a disease. Besides all of that it depends on how many people that the both of you have slept with.

Just look at it as the both of you should go and get tested together. If you plan on being with each other for a while that is. Or is it that you just look at each other as a one night stand or a piece of meat? Because everyone knows that you purchase a piece of meat from a food store.

Real talk is that some women are too afraid to commit to anything. Too afraid to commit to themselves first. Too afraid to commit to any kind of relationship. Too afraid to be committed to their job. And finally too afraid to commit to being able to love or trust anyone.

Real talk is that sometimes all it takes is faith and hope. Hope that all the pain will just go away. Faith in the man above that he will send someone your way that doesn't mind showing you off to his friends because he loves you. Someone who is there to catch you when you fall. Someone who is like a protection shield.

As human beings in the world today we fail to realize that we are our own enemy. That money is the root to all evil. We are always trying to tell someone who they should or shouldn't date. We are also always trying to give someone the wrong advice. But it doesn't always hurt to listen to someone who has a little bit more experience then you do. But what doesn't always hurt you only makes you stronger.

Let's just say if a woman had two best friends who does she believe when it comes down to it in the end? Does she believe the person that she has known the longest ? Or does she believe someone that she has just met? In any kind of situation she should believe the person that she has known the longest. Because a total stranger will tell you anything just to be your friend.

Life sometimes is just like a sitcom. Words that you want for a person to say. Sitcom is just targeted conversation. And dialogue is just a line and a response. It is like if you were to put a actress next to a normal person. Who would you believe that would get the lead part in a movie? The actress would be the one to get the part depending on if the normal person hasn't studied just as hard for the same part.

The only thing that some of us as humans know how to do is just fight, kill and hate each other for all sorts of reasons. Whether it be for a reasonable reason or a stupid one. Some people just don't know how to settle their differences by trying to work things out with each other. Instead of having to deal with baby mama or baby daddy drama each and everyday.

Some peoples life is just like well I am living and that is all that matters. But for someone to love them and think of them everyday is what keeps a smile on their face. I feel like a happy person is a person that you might never have to worry about crying over something.

People cry because they get emotional. People cry when they are abused by someone. People feel like committing suicide when there is no one that wants to even give them a slice of bread.

I know that some of you are saying to yourself that I am tired of hearing her talk about real talk. You are wanting to hear more juicy gossip. It's like a woman knows when to draw the line. That certain things shouldn't be talked about like her sex life. But the deal is that you have some women that don't mind telling it all.

With some women you find that they would tell you every little thing that is going on down to the last detail. But I am here to say that I am not one of those women. I am not that open-minded. Whenever you find a woman doing that then it is time for you to your separate ways because she will tell even if you were messing with her best friend.

I am only being a believer of knowing what to do and what not to do. Because if you don't have trust or honesty in any relationship then you are just like a blank page. A blank page with no words on it because you have trust issues. Or you're not use to thinking for yourself.

If a person is not use to thinking for themselves then someone has to do their thinking for them. Or as someone might say that they have brain fart. That they have selective memory. They only remember what they want to remember. They only plan things one day at a time. When some people are just living for today and hoping to see another day.

But when you have someone that wants to argue with you and miss you afterwards that can be kind of odd. It's like if someone tried to run a train on you at a motel. You might either go for it or you might try to kill someone in order for you to survive. But you don't think that at the time that your freedom is the most important thing to you.

That's because in this world you have several types of people. You have those that knows what it means to have everything that they ever wanted. And you have those that have to work for what they want and try to keep it.

A blank mind is a mind without thoughts. A mind without thoughts is a mind that is just thoughtless. And the only way for it to be able to live again is that you have to be reminded of the important things to do. Because it is more easy for a person to give up then for them to sit up and say I'm sorry.

Some women think that they have given a man so many years of their life that they just want to be alone or given another chance. One more chance to understand them mentally and not hurt them physically. Forgiveness only goes a long way if you allow it to. But some people are so weak that they just give in to anything.

It's like the saying goes that silence is golden. Or treat a woman like you would treat your mother or grandmother. Is that with respect of her wishes? Or do you disrespect her and low grade her feelings and appearance? If you care for her you wouldn't let anything happen to her.

Real talk is all about the truth and some lies depending on who the person is. But 90% of the time you are hoping for the truth. The other 10% the time those little white lies adds up to one big lie. Someone ends up with a broken heart. Or even worse they will slice your tires or throw a brick thru your window.

It is like saying that I don't believe in the saying love them and then leave them. Because some people find themselves to attached. Some of them are willing to sit down and talk. But they want to do it when it is too late. As you are leaving out the door with your head down. Or maybe held up high.

Most men feel like they don't mind their mate posing nude for the camera. That's because in the world you have both jealous men and women. They feel like they have to control your every move. From going to the bathroom down to going to work. Real talk is that some women are so spoiled.

A spoiled woman is a woman that is so use to having her man do anything for her. But what a woman fails to realize is that a man can be just as spoiled as her. A spoiled woman wants her way right on the spot. If not she feels like she can go elsewhere to get what she wants.

Real talk is that women of today just need to learn how to love themselves first before they can love anyone else. That is because everyday that goes by so many people are dying. Both young and old. Some of them dying from natural causes and others are dying by the bare hands of a angry person. That is because some people are not thankful for what they have. Or for who they have in their life. That is because love can make people do some crazy things.

Real talk is that people just don't believe in prayer. They are just non-believers. It is like saying that they are a Jehovah witness. But there are also a lot of different religions also. It is like saying if a person was in another country and they did something wrong that their hand would be cut off.

Real talk is that some people can go from doing drugs to going to a major change in their life. For some people life is like an hour glass. You never know when your time is up. It is like saying here today and gone tomorrow or within minutes. It is like saying that a person's life has just flashed before their eyes. Only if life was just peaches and cream. But we haven't achieved all that we have wanted to as humans. We still have some racial problems in some states. The majority of black history has been taken out of our school books. We only know so much as humans but not as much as we ought to know.

The moral of this chapter is to advise us as human beings of what signs that we should look for when it comes to wanting to be happy and loving yourself first.

Chapter Four

A woman wants for her man not only to be her lover but to also be her friend. To be her soul mate. To be her companion. A woman wants her man just to cuddle up next to her. Some women just want to be loved and not be made love to. Being that it is hard for some people to understand. Because you have some women that feel like they need some kind of male figure to confine in.

What a woman really wants is just to be understood. She might want a candle light dinner every now and then. She might want to lay her head on your lap. Or she might want you to lay your head in between her breast. A woman just wants for a man not to look at her as his boy toy or some kind of sex object. But a woman just wants to be treated with respect.

This is what any average woman might want. She might want a man to watch lifetime with her while she whispers sweet nothings in his ear. Some women might want a man to leave a passion mark some where on them. And you have some women that have out grown those things called passion marks.

A woman just wants to feel appreciated. Every time a man makes his woman feel appreciated is everyday that he will be treated with respect and not treated like some mama's boy. But if she is only appreciated 2 or 3 times out of a year then that might spell trouble for you. Trouble that you as the man are going to be deep in the dog house.

If a man ends up in the dog house he has to work really hard to get out. Here's what he might do; buy you two dozen roses, buy you the most expensive chocolate candy, buy you a 24 karat gold diamond ring, a new car or truck or just leave. Because most men feel like the only thing they should have to do is try to work it out. For example, he might feel like he is spoiling you.

Only because if a man spoils a woman she will always expect to be spoiled by everyone after you. Even if things don't seem to work out for the both of you in the near future. One man isn't going to spoil you or wine and dine you just because every other man you had did it. But you have some women that are just glad that you are their company. They just want to sit near the fireside. Or maybe they just want to sit in the hot tub with you.

For example there is girl that I know that seems to be confused. She says that she is in the process of getting a divorce. That her husband wasn't keeping her happy. So she said that it is okay to have a backup plan. But her idea of a backup plan is to have male friends with benefits. Seems like she needs some kind of reality check.

It's because in life you have women that know what they want. And there are those that think that they know but really aren't so sure. They don't know if they want security or just want you as their sleeping buddy. Although, I know of another person that doesn't want to admit that she needs help.

Exactly what is a woman that needs help? A woman that needs to mind her own business and quit worrying about other people. She is a woman that has problems of her own but yet she tries to cover them up. She is also a woman that looks to start an argument. But the deal is that someone has to be the bigger woman and just walk away.

It's like saying in reality that women gossip too much. Some of them just do it for the attention. When the other half really know how to honor their mate's wishes. A prime example is that you find men saying I love you more often then a woman would. But someone told me that if you find a woman saying it more then a man does then she's being insecure.

An insecure woman is only trying to make sure that you don't communicate with anyone that she doesn't know. She wants to always be in the spotlight. Not wanting to share you with anyone else. Not wanting to let you except any gifts from any other woman. Especially if it is something as simple as a plate of food. That's just a sign that she is afraid of losing you to another woman. It's like saying that she is doing her wifely duties. Or like saying that the grass is greener on the other side.

The grass is greener on the other side means man wise. When a woman crosses over to the other side of the tracks. She then realizes that she misses you and that her new boyfriend treats her like dirt. Although, she might want to call you up and try to apologize asking you to give her another chance.

Here's what a woman might do if you gave her a second chance; she will give you some breathing space, learn to trust you more, cook for you more often rub your feet and or maybe wash your dirty laundry. She might also treat you like a king and not a little prince.

But we all know that finding that kind of a woman could be really impossible. It's like saying that a man just has to settle for a less then average woman. A woman that doesn't act like a wanna be diva. A woman that doesn't want to be intimate every minute of the hour. Although, you have some women that want some men to undress them with their eyes.

I bet you are wondering now how does a man undress a woman with his eyes? First he gives her that certain look in her eyes. Then he moves on to the middle part of her body. Finally he reaches the last part of her body and before you know it she is in your bedroom waiting on you. She might have some desserts waiting also.

After you reach the bedroom the both of you might start from the floor leading up to the bed. But before he begins he might ask you to slip into something revealing so he can pour some Hershey syrup on you. Then he will finish by putting on the toppings. Afterwards the two of you begin to get down to business.

After everything is said and done the both of you begin to lead to the shower and proceed to cleaning up each other. Once the two of you are finished taking a shower together your man might fix you a full course dinner. After you digest your food you might go to sleep or begin to watch the sports channel with your man. That's if he doesn't watch what you want to watch.

I bet some of you are saying that was so romantic. Or maybe you are saying that they did it because it might have been nothing else on t.v. to watch. That's because some people don't know how to be romantic. Or either that their love sparks can only be lit by a certain person. But you have some people that don't care who they sleep with.

That leading up to saying that some women just want a man to train. Because if a woman feels like she has got a man trained then she thinks that she is in control. It's like he is under her spell. But what some women fail to realize is that a man isn't going to always be there to pick you up when you fall. It's like saying once a cheat always a cheat.

That's only because some women know when some men are up to no good. But you have some women that will except you back even after you've cheated. Although, there are signs of a cheater. They will stay out all night and won't answer their cell phone. Another thing is that when they get to the house they will head straight to the shower, try to scrub away another woman's perfume and then go straight to sleep.

Besides in life you have some single women that get so drunk that they will end up sleeping with a total stranger. Then after maybe using no protection at all they might end up pregnant a week later. So, how is it that I think that I know what women want ? I observe and besides I am a woman myself.

For example, you have women that just take love for granted. They feel like they are gods gift to men. Like they can have any man that they want. Or that they can just take over the streets. It is like saying that some women need a man to pay their bills. Or they need a man for comfort.

Women just want to feel like they are not in it alone. That they are not in it to win it. For example, I feel like if certain women took a look at another person's mistakes that they would learn a thing or two. Women just want to be able to get along with each other. It's like saying that you don't know who to trust or who is really your friend. Because you have people that are just plan backstabbers. They just don't want to be happy for you.

It's like saying that you have to pay a person to be your friend. And when your money runs out your friendship with that person runs dry. Women just hate to see other women go up the letter of success. But when the shoe is on the other foot nothing would seem to be wrong then. It is as if a man would need a roadmap to know exactly what to do when it comes down to a woman.

Some women just feel like they just want to take life one day at a time. They feel like life is just one big joke. It is like some of them don't have any respect or dignity left in them. Like some of them just have to turn to drugs in order for them to calm down. For example, some women can take care of their children and have some alone time to do whatever they want.

That's only because I know of this woman that felt like her man had to eat before her kids. Her kids were afraid of being at home when her boyfriend was there in the living room. Because she felt like it was okay for her daughter to just skip town and supposedly go to a basketball game. But what she really did was went over her little boyfriend house and didn't anyone know her whereabouts until 24 hours later. She also felt like it was okay for her daughter to jump out of a school window. That she could have boys over her house but they had to be outside in the front yard.

The only good outcome is that she didn't end up pregnant. But it almost happened to her. She had her little sister lying for her. She had her sister to tell their mother that she went over her best friend house. When really her little sister had to ride her bike over her best friend's house to find out that she wasn't there. She was told that her sister hadn't been there all day. The little girls mother told her that she should check around the corner and maybe she would find them.

Women that don't know how to keep their teenage daughters out of trouble is just women that have no self control. It's like their dreams had to be sat aside just for their daughter to have some kind of future. But when you have your own child messing up then you should tell them that they have to make a decision. They should act right and learn to respect adults. Or they can just find somewhere else to stay.

But when a parent doesn't know to be a role model and show their children what's right and wrong then someone needs counseling. Although, you will always have someone in your family playing the I'm better then you game. Blood isn't always thicker then water. And family doesn't always stick up for each other especially when they are in the wrong. Because family is always the first ones to try to judge a book by its cover. Just like family is always the first ones calling you whenever something goes wrong with them.

That is why some women felt like they had to run away at a young age. But somehow the tables have made a turn and now it is your own child doing it to you. Not so funny is now what you're thinking. But you should always think about what you say before you say it. That's because people have feelings and by them being hurt all the time isn't going to help you at all. Women should just let their children make their own mistakes until they get grown and on their own. But you have some women that feel like they just have to always protect their children. Like they are suppose to always solve every problem that they have.

Some women know how to keep it real. But you also have some women that are just to open-minded. They should just be like a mime and not have a word to say at all. Because like the saying goes silence is golden. Children should be seen but not heard. They know that they should be somewhere in the house playing with children their own age. But they feel like if they see someone else child acting a certain way that it is okay for them to do it.

Although, whenever you see someone trying to play house you think to yourself should I step in? Or should I just let things continue as they are? But no matter decision that I make I hope that it wouldn't effect how things are between us is what you are thinking. It's not like you need someone to be your daddy. Or that you need someone to bail you out of trouble whenever you get in it.

Women just want to feel like they shouldn't have to eat just to solve every problem that they have. They also don't want to feel like they have to cry just to get over you. Either you are completely over them or you just hate to see them with someone else. Because true love only comes once maybe twice out of a lifetime. But it is like having a little pet name for your mate.

Although, whenever you have little pet or food names for your mate some people might find that a little cute. Or maybe they are just so stuck up on themselves that they don't have time to think. People that have time to think is people that are climbing the road to success. But whenever you have people worrying about other people business then it is time to move on.

So the moral to this chapter is to make sure you know what you are getting into before you do it.

Chapter Five

The worse thing that a woman could ever have to do is face the truth. She feels like she doesn't have to face her fears. Because she might be tired of running and being called a scary cat. Only because she feels like it is her turn to be taken care of. She might feel like no one cares about her at all.

For example, my boyfriend and I were just coming over the Chicago bridge proceeding to McDonalds. Although, as my boyfriend and I were proceeding to the door we witnessed a car accident. There was this man driving a blue van and he hit these people that were in a black car. He didn't look before he bagged out into the street.

The point is that driving down any street in Chicago is very dangerous. You get stuck in a traffic jam for almost an hour. And then you have people that try to cut in line just to get to the front of the line. But the deal is that I hope that elderly woman was okay. She was just very shaken up because it happened so fast. Although the police, ambulance, fire truck and others arrived at the scene within ten to fifteen minutes.

I know that whenever someone's life flashes before their eyes that someone has to take the responsibility for it. Although, the consequences would be that someone has to pay for someone else medical bills. Or even worse it could end up being their funeral expenses. That's because I see just so many accidents happen just about every other day.

Some accidents happen as a result of carelessness. Because just Wednesday night in Calumet, Illinois a woman lost her fiancé just as they were riding down the street and someone opened fire. But the bad part about it was that the law wasn't so quick to investigate on who did it.

Like the saying goes here today gone tomorrow. Tomorrow isn't promised to anyone. No one is guaranteed to live forever. But it is like saying that some people don't like the color of their skin. It is like saying that you have to be a certain color to make millions of dollars.

Although what men and women don't realize is that in some states there is still some people living in segregation. They have to be told what to do and when to do it. When to sleep and when not to sleep. But some of them would just rather die.

Besides the fact that it was one time when women couldn't vote. When African Americans weren't aloud to learn how to read or write. They weren't even aloud to go to the same schools as whites. They weren't aloud to participate in any kind of sports. They were not also aloud to eat at the same restaurants or go to a motel if they went on a vacation.

As humans of this generation we just hate to bare the fact that we should be lucky to do certain things. Like go to school and get an education. Not have to worry about seeing signs that say colored and white. But the bad thing is that black history isn't taught the way that it should be. We are only taught so much by reading about it.

You have some people that feel like they should be treated as equal as the next person. Whether it is a woman doing a man's job better then he can. Or it is a man telling his woman to stay at home. That she don't have to worry about a thing. He tells her that everything is under control.

A prime example of that is what I heard on the radio Thursday morning. It was a Chicago station. This woman told her husband that he didn't have to work. She said that she makes enough money to take care of the both of them. Some of you might feel like man he is lucky to have her as his wife. Or at least he should be if he is not using her and taking advantage of her.

A lucky person that is with another person should just hold on to them. Because if that person slips up once it's like saying you're gone. Or do you love him that much that you just take him back. No matter what anyone has to say are you just that strong? Or do you let him go?

A person's freedom is the best thing that they could ever have. But when you lost your freedom you can't ask for anything else. It is like separating a child from its favorite stuffed animal. Or telling your mate that you don't love him anymore.

Things aren't given to anyone on a silver platter. You have to give respect in order to get respect. You have to compromise in order to be able to move on with your relationship. You have to forgive and forget. Remember where you came from. Whether it was from the hood or from bel-air. People make a living the best way that they can.

For example, it is like saying that you had no childhood. Or that you find it hard to love or trust any man. It is like this girl that I know who couldn't trust her uncle. Because her uncle tried to tamper with her body. Why would anyone go that far as to do such a thing like that? Because they don't want to love anyone else outside of their family I guess.

As a result of that he felt so guilty about doing what he did that he chose to move. But the woman didn't think that he would move because his family stays here. But until this day she seems to be so confused about men. She has to drink in order to try and forget about what happened.

Although, whenever you find a person that is too generous and giving you should check their background out. You shouldn't have to watch any movies to give you any ideas. You should already know what to do. You should know if someone is sleeping with your man. Or if you are just so concerned about everything that goes on.

Some women just find themselves in the wrong place at the wrong time. They feel like they need some kind of guidance. Like they just want you to give them that extra push. That's because some women are like fireworks. If you say the wrong thing to them they are bound to explode.

Whenever you find an explosive woman don't run from her. You should sit down and learn a few things from them. Happiness only goes so far. And that you see why they can't keep a man. Because their mouth won't allow them to do so. They want things done their way or it will be the high way for you.

Women shouldn't have to be enemies with each other. We shouldn't have to be enemies with our men. But we should think about what we are doing before we do it. We should stand on our own two feet. And not feel like we should need a man to validate us. Independent women are more successful by making their own money and not needing anyone to pay their bills.

Some women just worry too much. When you have some men that will just get over it and move on. Women don't know how to settle their differences and say I'm sorry. They would just rather go on with their life feeling lonely. Or trying to find someone to have and to hold in the middle of the night.

Some women just want to be a hustler. They want to have their cake and eat it too. They find it hard to want to listen to what an older person has to say. They are always jumping to conclusions. They pretend that they really want you. When the only thing that they want is for you to buy them something.

Some women are just more emotional then other women. It just takes longer for some of them to heal. It is like when a woman sees something that she wants. She would do anything to get her hands on it. Even if you are with another woman she just feels like she isn't doing her job right. Or maybe you should just start off by getting his name and number.

In conclusion it is better to leave a woman alone especially when it is that time of the month. But love just ain't the way that it use to be. You just don't find relationships lasting for 60 or more years. They just don't follow their vowels by the part of saying for sickness and in health until death do us part.

POETRY SECTION

10 Ways to Commit

In today's society there are a million of ways to be committed to . . .

1). Cook your man breakfast in bed.
2). Tell him how much you love him.
3). Don't be afraid to tell him your deepest inner thoughts.
4). Run him some bath water.
5). Agree to disagree when it comes down to minor things in a relationship.
6). Wash his dishes for him while holding a conversation with him and listening to music at the same time.
7). Do your laundry together.
8). Cuddle up next to your man and try to be a little romantic and less intimate.
9). Watch some of his favorite television shows and he might return the favor.
10). Try to get along with his friends without trying to be such a big flirt.

So without a doubt of committing think to yourself is he really worth it or can I do better?

10 Signs of a Married Cheater

Although there are a million ways to tell if a married person is cheating here are a few.

1) you have to screen their phone calls.
2) they lie to you about where they're going or where they've been.
3) they can't tell you where their wedding ring is at.
4) they hang around a lot of single people.
5) they will mess up your credit and you wouldn't know anything about it until you try to go and get something for yourself.
6) they might have another married person meet them at a certain place.
7) they will come home and jump straight in the shower.
8) you see a videotape of them being on cheaters.
9) you allow them to have too much freedom and alone time to themselves without you being their by their side and showing them some kind of attention and affection.
10) you will find a pack of condoms in their wallet and you know that they are not being used on you and then the condoms might have a phone number on it.

A Wanna be Diva

A wanna be diva is a woman that just wants to hustle.
A wanna be diva wears tight little clothes. A wanna be diva just runs the
streets all of the time.
A wanna be diva is always so stuck up on themselves that they don't
even have time to say hi.
A wanna be diva wears those flashy sunglasses. A wanna be diva should
be someone that shouldn't have to ask for anything.
That is because they should be able to make their own money no matter
what the case maybe.

A wanna be diva will take almost any man for granted.
A wanna be diva knows how to keep her own vehicle under any
circumstances.
A wanna be diva wouldn't get their hair and nails done just to end up in
a cat fight later.
A wanna be diva is a materialistic woman. A wanna be diva is a woman
that lives in a expensive house.
A wanna be diva doesn't need a man to validate her. A wanna be diva
doesn't need a man to pay her bills.

A wanna be diva is a woman that should know what it means to take a
vacation with her man.
A wanna be diva is afraid to let a real man love her.
A wanna be diva is a person that has a very feisty attitude towards
anyone or anything.
A wanna be diva is a woman that doesn't need help from anyone if she
has a flat tire.
Or even if she runs out of gas. A wanna be diva is a woman that should
know how to cook.

Compatibility and Communication

Compatibility and communication is the number one key to a successful
relationship. It's like without one how could you have the other.
Compatibility is something that the two of you should have in common.
Communication is another important factor to consider when you are in
relationship with anyone.
Communicating is being able to open up and let your partner know
your most inner thoughts.

Without communication in any relationship everything might go down
hill from there. If something turns from good to bad in a relationship
you might not have a good future ahead.
It's like saying that a person needs some reassurance. Reassurance in
order to know what they want out of life.
For example, in life you have people that know the whole truth about
trying to tell a story.
And then you have certain people that think
that they know the whole truth.

That is why anyone that is a couple should take time out to talk to each
other whenever anything is going wrong. Communication with your
relatives can also be a very risky thing also. Only because you have some
relatives in life that loves to just stretch the truth to make their
story look good.
But in life sometimes you have some people that live by the words
of silence is golden.
Although, I feel like I don't have to get even with violence.
I get even with words.

So this is a message to everyone out there in the world who knows what it
feels like to be pretended to be liked. I feel like if you don't like someone
or what they are doing then the best thing for you to do is just go on with
your own life and just be happy for them. Besides the fact that money is
the root of all evil. Certain relatives and people you associate with are the
first ones to stab you in the back.